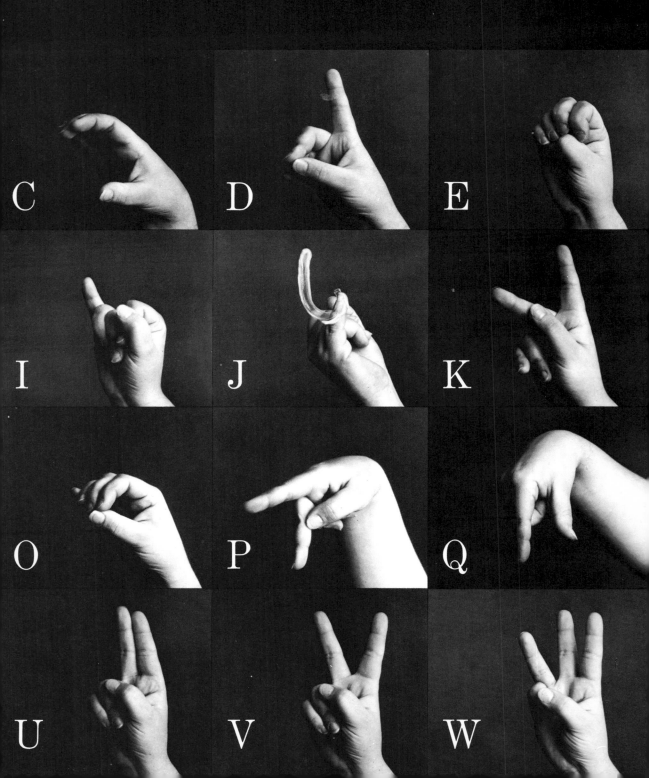

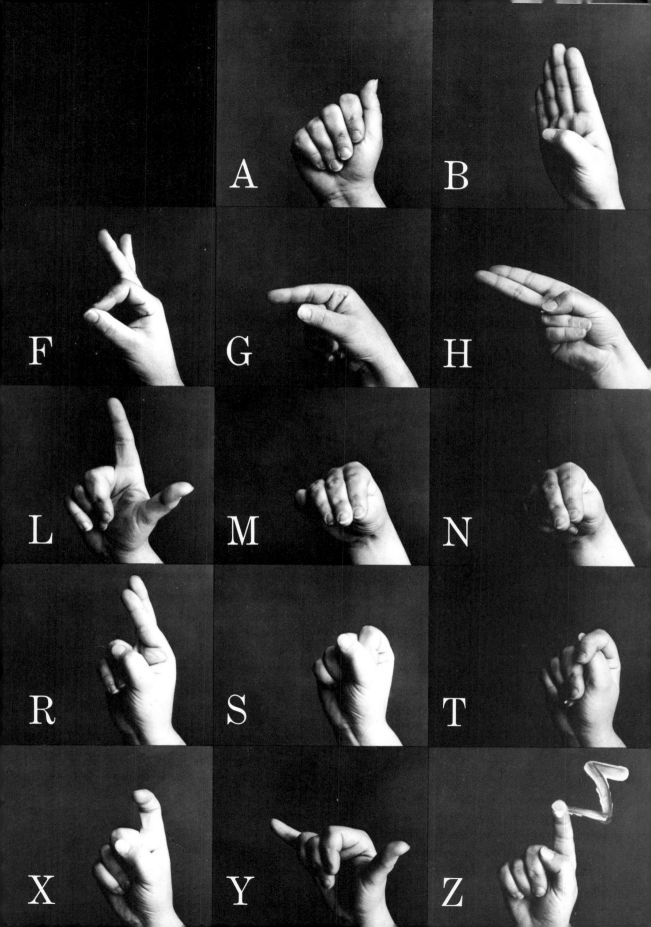

YOU DON'T HAVE TO USE YOUR VOICE TO TALK. YOU CAN TALK WITH YOUR EYES, YOUR FACE, YOUR HANDS, YOUR BODY.

THE AMERICAN INDIANS USED TO TALK THIS WAY WHEN THEY DIDN'T KNOW THE LANGUAGE OF ANOTHER TRIBE.

THIS IS THE FIRST BOOK OF ITS KIND FOR YOUNG PEOPLE ON TWO WAYS THAT DEAF PEOPLE TALK: *FINGER SPELLING,* FORMING WORDS LETTER BY LETTER WITH THE FINGERS OF ONE HAND, AND *SIGNING,* MAKING A PICTURE OR SIGN WITH ONE OR TWO HANDS FOR EACH WORD OR IDEA.

YOU ALREADY KNOW MANY *HANDTALK* SIGNS IN THIS BOOK, LIKE *BIG, CRAZY, HELLO.*

A SIGN STANDS FOR THE CONCEPT BEHIND THE WORD AS WELL AS THE WORD ITSELF, SO THAT YOU CAN MAKE *BIG* ALSO MEAN *LARGE, HUGE, ENORMOUS, GIGANTIC,* BY CHANGING THE FEELING OF THE GESTURE. DON'T BE AFRAID TO USE YOUR EYES, FACE, BODY, AND YOUR LEGS TO SHOW EXACTLY WHAT YOU MEAN.

SIGNS CHANGE WITH THE TIMES, AS WELL AS FROM PLACE TO PLACE. THE OLD SIGN FOR *TELEPHONE* USED TO BE MADE WITH TWO HANDS, ONE AT THE EAR AND ONE AT THE MOUTH. SOME PEOPLE DO *VAMPIRE* BY PLACING THE TWO FINGERS OF THE LETTER *V* TO THE SIDE OF THE NECK. THE SIGN FOR *AMERICA* IS DONE DIFFERENTLY IN ENGLAND, FRANCE, THE SOVIET UNION, AND THE UNITED STATES.

THE *HANDTALK* WORDS IN THIS BOOK ARE SIMPLE AND FUN TO DO. TRY THEM WITH A FRIEND, AND MAKE UP SOME NEW SIGNS IF YOU WANT TO HAVE A SECRET CODE. NOW YOU CAN TALK FROM FAR AWAY WITHOUT SHOUTING, FROM BEHIND CLOSED WINDOWS, AND EVEN UNDER WATER.

THIS IS ONLY A BEGINNING. THERE ARE OVER 5,000 SIGNS IN THE LANGUAGE OF THE DEAF. IT IS A RICH AND BEAUTIFUL LANGUAGE USED BY HUNDREDS OF THOUSANDS IN THE UNITED STATES ALONE.

IF YOU WANT TO LEARN MORE *HANDTALK* ASK A DEAF PERSON WHO KNOWS SIGN LANGUAGE TO SHOW YOU.

THIS WORK WAS MADE POSSIBLE THROUGH THE GENEROUS COOPERATION OF THE NATIONAL THEATRE OF THE DEAF AND THE EUGENE O'NEILL MEMORIAL THEATER CENTER, INC. THE NATIONAL THEATRE OF THE DEAF IS FUNDED, PRIMARILY, BY THE U.S. OFFICE OF EDUCATION, DEPARTMENT OF HEALTH, EDUCATION AND WELFARE. ALSO, THANKS TO TIMOTHY SCANLON, FREDA NORMAN, JOSEPH SARPY, DOROTHY MILES, FANNY YEH, ARTHUR TOMLINSON, MAX BURGESS, GUY WONDER AND ESPECIALLY NIKKI KILPATRICK AND DAVID HAYS, DIRECTOR OF NTD.

HANDTALK

AN ABC OF FINGER SPELLING & SIGN LANGUAGE

REMY CHARLIP   MARY BETH   GEORGE ANCONA

FOUR WINDS PRESS   Macmillan Publishing Company   New York

Text copyright © 1974 by Remy Charlip and Mary Beth Miller
Illustrations copyright © 1974 by Remy Charlip
Photographs copyright © 1974 by George Ancona
Aladdin Books
Macmillan Publishing Company
866 Third Avenue, New York, NY 10022
Collier Macmillan Canada, Inc.
First Aladdin Books Edition 1986
Printed in the United States of America
A hardcover edition of Handtalk *is available from Four Winds Press,*
Macmillan Publishing Company.

10 9 8 7 6 5 4

LIBRARY OF CONGRESS CATALOGING-IN-PUBLICATION DATA
Charlip, Remy.
    Handtalk: an ABC of finger spelling & sign language.
    Originally published: New York: Parents' Magazine Press, c1974.
    Summary: An introduction to two kinds of sign language: finger
spelling, or forming words letter by letter with the fingers, and signing,' or
making signs with one or two hands for each word or idea.
    1. Sign language—Juvenile literature. [1. Sign language. 2. Alphabet]
I. Mary Beth. II. Ancona, George. III. Title. IV. Title: Hand talk.
HV2476.C47   1987   86-20585 ISBN 0-689-71108-5 (pbk.)

FOR MY FATHER CHESTER, MY MOTHER NELLIE, MY SISTER BEVERLY

A

ANGEL

B

BUTTER

C

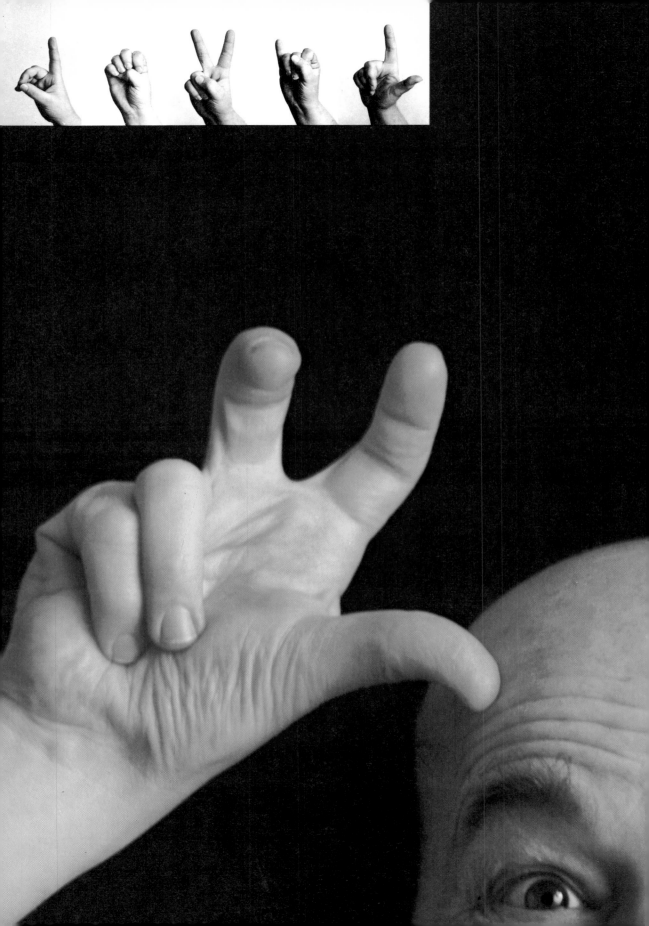

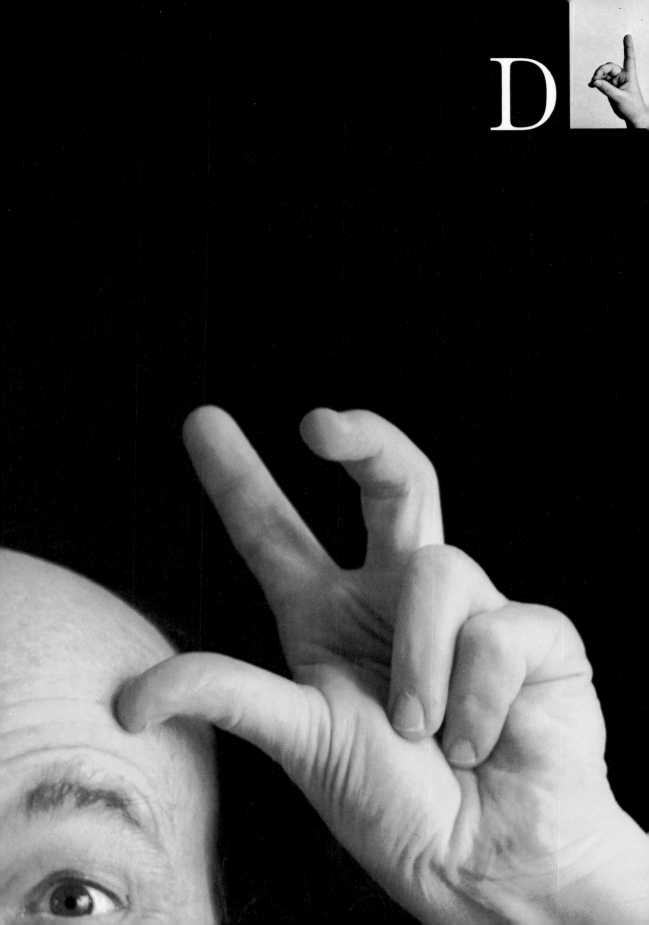

D

E

F

G

H

I

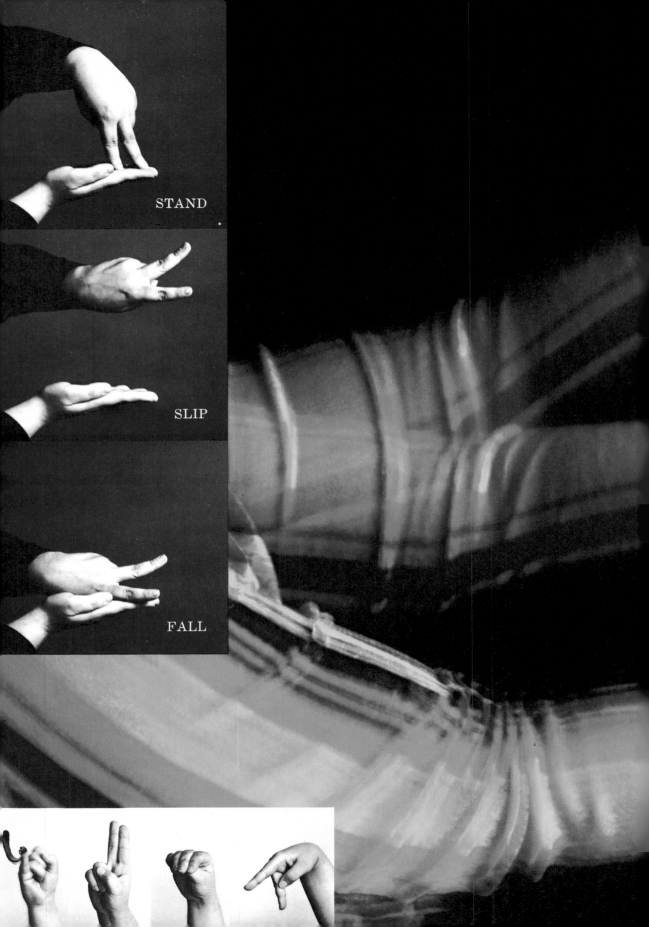

STAND

SLIP

FALL

J

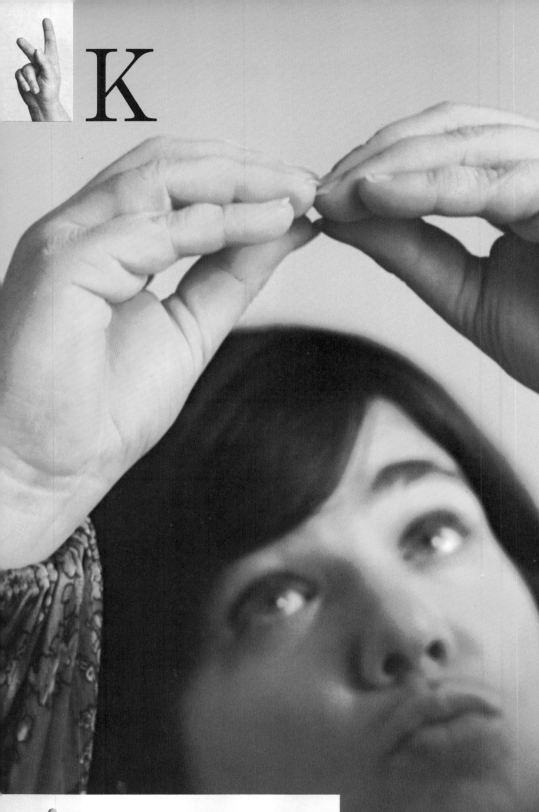

K

L

M

 N

TAP THE TIPS OF THE 3 FINGERS YOU USE TO MAKE

NO

NO

NO

O

THE LETTER N AND YOU GET THE WORD NO.   O.K.?

NO

O

K

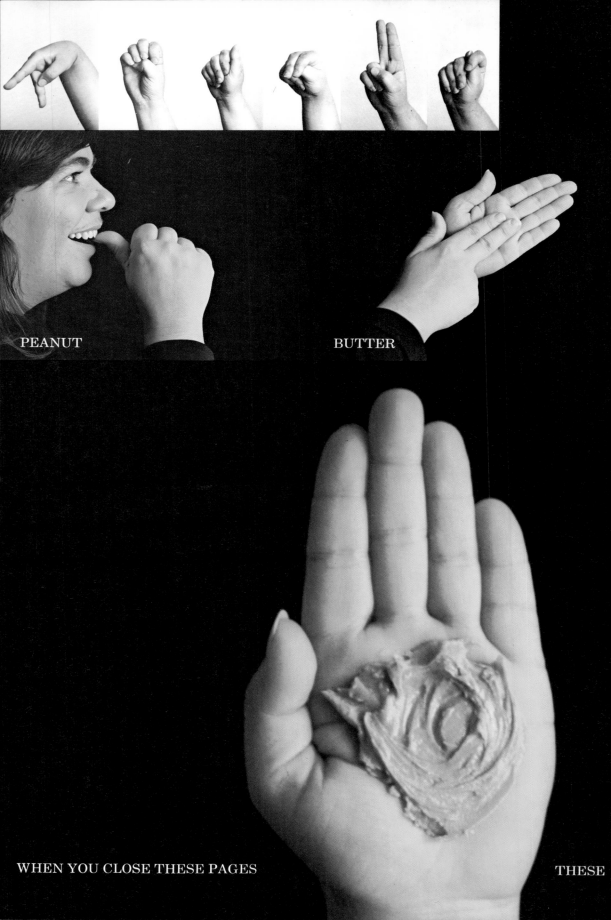

PEANUT

BUTTER

WHEN YOU CLOSE THESE PAGES

THESE

P

AND

JELLY

HANDS

MAKE THE SIGN FOR SANDWICH

Q

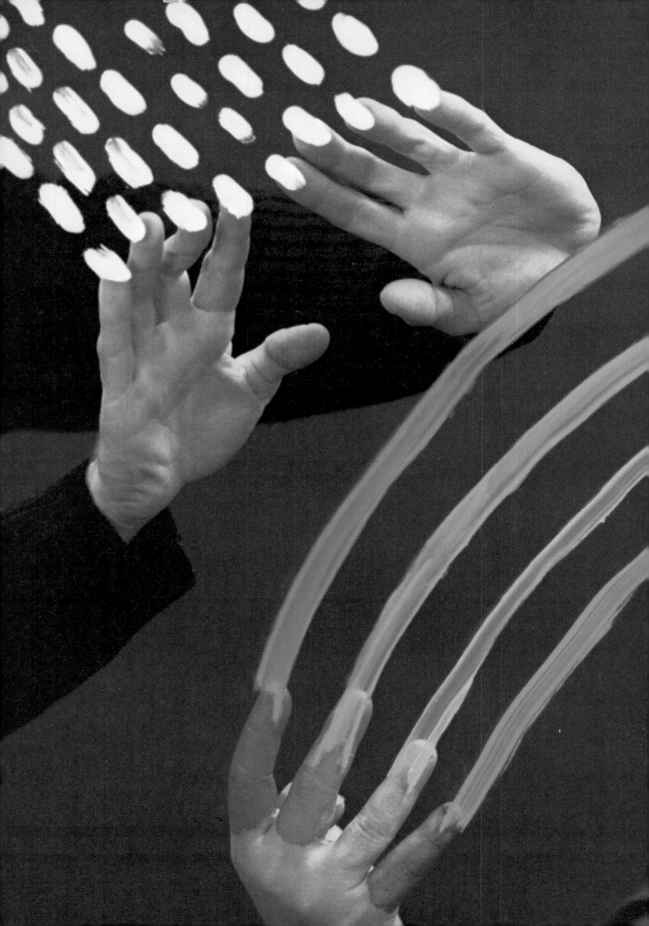

R

To Rita   Love Mary Beth

S

CIRCLE WITH FINGER, THEN OPEN SAME HAND

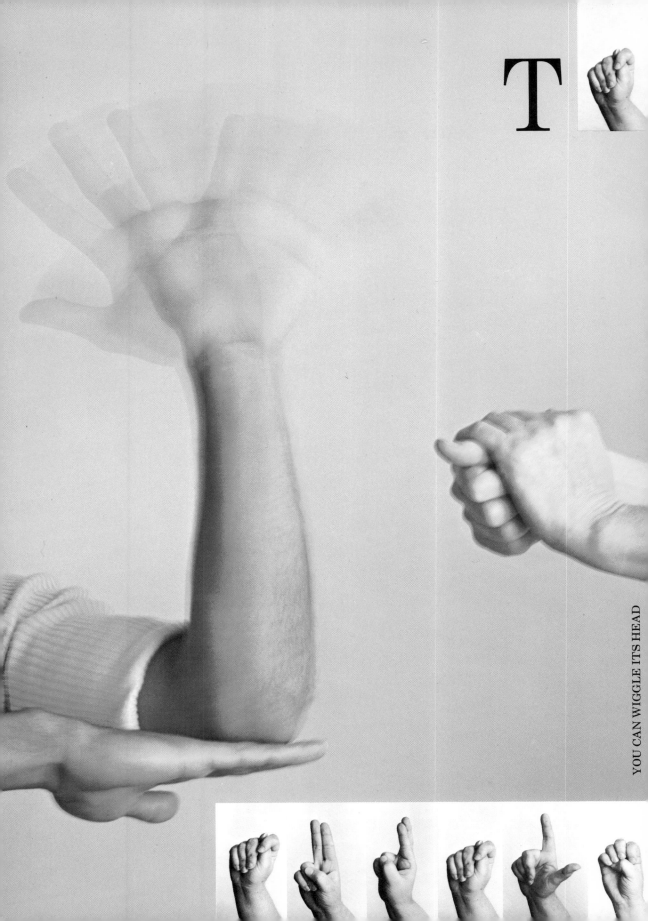

T

YOU CAN WIGGLE ITS HEAD

U

IN A VERY UGLY VILLAGE

NEAR A VERY UGLY VALLEY

UNDER A VERY UGLY VOLCANO

LIVED A VERY UGLY VAMPIRE

WITH HIS BEAUTIFUL VULTURE

MY NAME IS VALENTINE

W

OPEN AND CLOSE THE FINGERS OF ONE HAND LIKE THE SHUTTER
OF A CAMERA. IT IS ALSO THE SIGN FOR A FLASH OF LIGHT.

X

I

L

Y

COMBINE 3 LETTERS FOR SHORTHAND: I LOVE YOU

Y

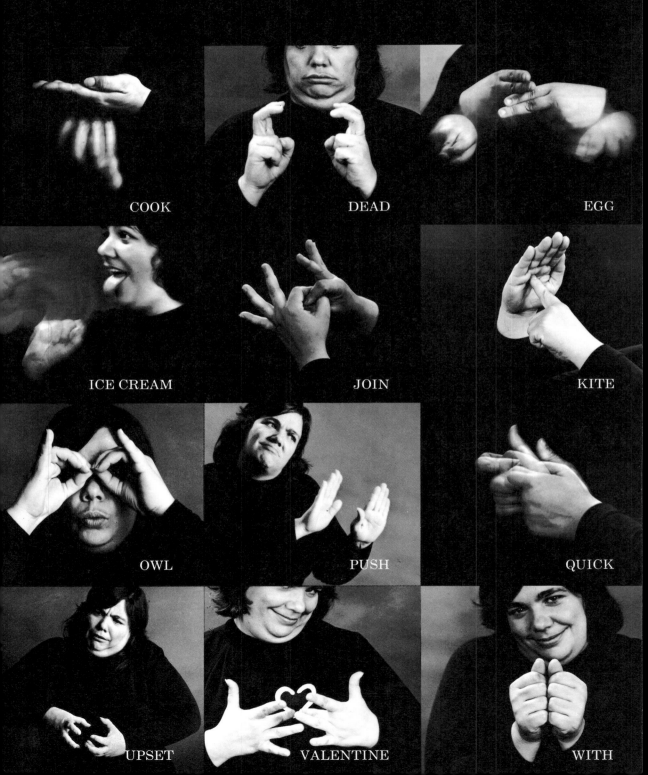

SIGNING: WITH ONE OR TWO HANDS MAKE A
SIGN OR PICTURE FOR EACH WORD OR IDEA.

COOK

DEAD

EGG

ICE CREAM

JOIN

KITE

OWL

PUSH

QUICK

UPSET

VALENTINE

WITH

ALLIGATOR   BIG

FUNNY   GROW   HELLO

LAUGH   MY   NAME

READ   SAD   TELEPHONE

XYLOPHONE   YELL   ZERO